Houghton Mifflin

WELCOME
LITERACY ACTIVITY BOOK

Senior Authors
J. David Cooper
John J. Pikulski

Authors
Kathryn H. Au
Margarita Calderón
Jacqueline C. Comas
Marjorie Y. Lipson
J. Sabrina Mims
Susan E. Page
Sheila W. Valencia
MaryEllen Vogt

Consultants
Dolores Malcolm
Tina Saldivar
Shane Templeton

INVITATIONS TO LITERACY

Houghton Mifflin Company • Boston
Atlanta • Dallas • Geneva, Illinois • Palo Alto • Princeton

CONTENTS

Punchouts

MAGIC PICTURES

Consonant Sounds and Letters

Bb — bird

Cc — cat

Dd — dinosaur

Ff — fish

Gg — ghost

Hh — horse

Jj — jack-in-the-box

Kk — king

Ll — lion

Mm — monster

Nn — nurse

Pp — pig

Qq — queen

Rr — rocket

Ss — seal

Tt — tiger

Vv — vest

Ww — worm

Xx — x-ray

Yy — yarn

Zz — zebra

1

Vowel Sounds and Letters

Aa

alligator

acorn

Ee

elephant

eel

Ii
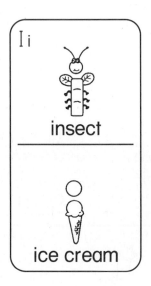

insect

ice cream

Oo

ostrich

ocean

Uu

umbrella

unicorn

Name

Show and Tell

 Add details to finish the picture.

 Then write about your picture.

SHOW AND TELL

Name

Good Morning!

b

Color the pictures whose names begin like 🐦.

Name

Find It!

✏️ Circle the word that names each picture.

LOST AND FOUND

ball
tack

bag
top

boat
tape

book
toy

🖍 Draw something whose name begins like  or 🐯 that might be in the Lost and Found.

✏️ Write the word that names
your picture.

_____

- - - - - - - - - - - - - - - - - -

 Off We Go—See What We Know! 7

Name

Field Trip

✏️

g

✏️ Draw a line from the big to the pictures

whose names begin like **goat**.

goat

Name

We Share Books

✏️ Draw a line from the big 🔤 to the pictures whose names begin like **vest**.

vest

✏️ Draw something whose name begins like 🔤.

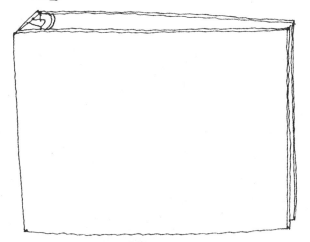

 Off We Go—See What We Know! **9**

Busy Day

✏️ **Think of each beginning sound. Write g or v.**

✏️ **Draw a line from each letter you wrote to the
correct lunch box.**

Name

What's for Lunch?

✏️ Draw a line from the picture to the word it goes with.

①

van

bat

③

take

gate

②

bird

girl

④

vine

time

🖍️ Draw something whose name begins like or that might be on a lunch box.

✏️ Write the word that names your picture.

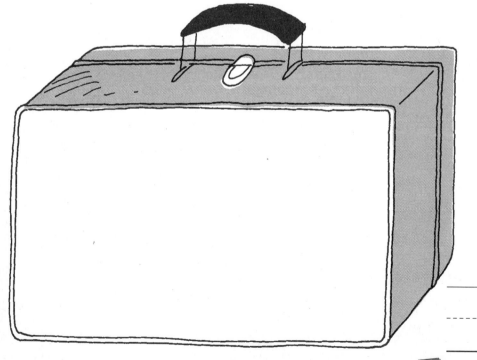

_____

- -

Off We Go—See What We Know!

11

Visit the Library

Trace the letters. Draw a line from each letter

to a picture whose name starts like  .

k   k   k   k   k

Name

Our Class Play

 Trace the letters. Draw a line from each letter

to a picture whose name starts like .

m   m   m   m   m

 Off We Go—See What We Know!   13

Name

Lining Up

✏️ **Trace the letters. Draw a line from each letter to a picture whose name starts with z.**

z   z   z   z   z

Name

Play Time

✏️ **Think of each beginning sound.**

Write k, m, or z.

✏️ **Draw a line from each letter you wrote to the correct ball.**

 Off We Go—See What We Know! **15**

Name

Keep Moving!

✏️ **Circle the word that names each picture.**

zip
get

tell
march

bake
kick

mix
tip

🖍️ **Draw something you can do in school whose name**

begins like 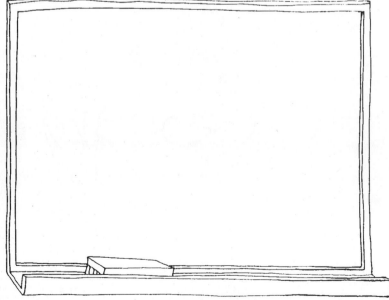 **,** , **or** **.**

✏️ **Write the word that names the action.**

4

I tip!

(Fold Line)

This Is My Book

_____

Kip

I bake.

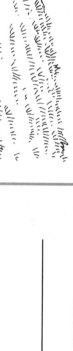

1

I jump.

Up, up, up . . .

3

(Fold Line)

I run.

2

Name

Run and Jump!

✂ **Cut out and paste each sentence next
to the picture it matches.**

1

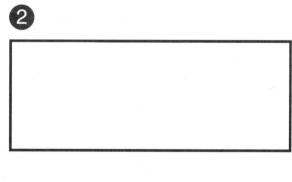

2

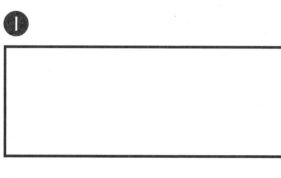

3

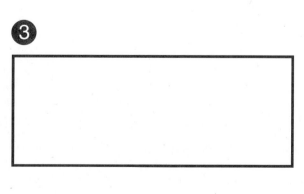

I jump all the time.

The  jump up.

All the  run.

Off We Go—See What We Know! **17**

Name _____

Behind the Barn

✏️ Draw a line to connect each speech
to the animal that is saying it.

I run up
the **dock**.

I make the
cook run.

I take the
corn.

✏️ Now label the pictures.

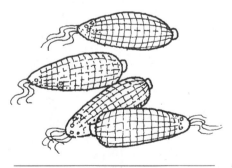

_____

_____

_____

Off We Go—See What We Know

25

Name

In the Yard

✏️ j

✏️ Circle and color the pictures whose names begin like .

Name

Farmer's Breakfast

✏ _____

p _____

✏ Circle and color the pictures whose names
begin like 🐷 .

Name

Rabbit's Chores

Circle and color the pictures whose names begin like  .

Name

Nesting Nellie

✏️

n

✏️ **Draw a line from Nellie to her nest. Connect the pictures whose names begin like** .

nest

Name

The Yak Farm

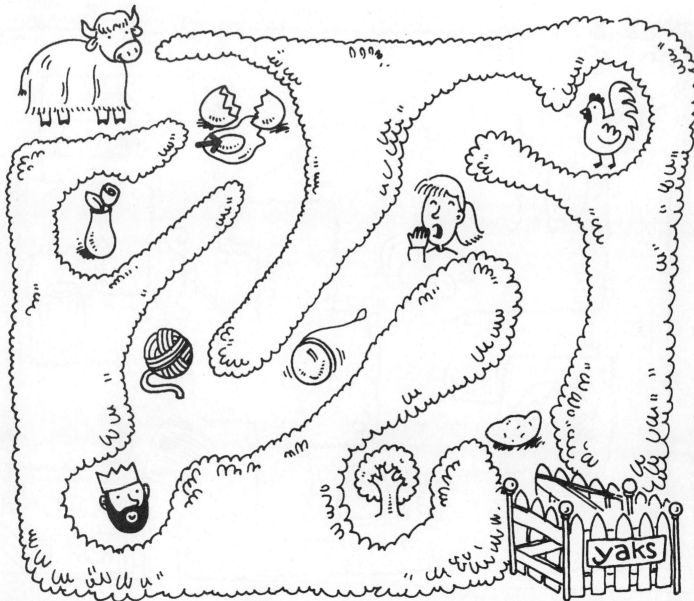

Draw a line from the yak to the pen. Connect the pictures whose names begin with **y**.

Name _____

What's in the Barn?

✏️ **Think of each beginning sound. Write n or y.**

🖍️ **Color green the pictures whose names begin like 👩‍⚕️ .**

Color yellow the pictures whose names begin like 🧶 .

Off We Go—See What We Know! **33**

Name

Farmhouse Food

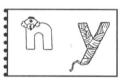

Read the story.

This takes two **yolks**.

Cat bakes all **night**.

Yum!   Yum!

Cat makes **noodles**.

Yawn.

Cat takes a **nap**.

Dog rakes the **yard**.

Draw a picture of something whose name begins like 👨‍⚕️

or 🧶 for the animals to eat.

Write the word that names your picture.

4

Pat and Jen went fast.

(Fold Line)

This Is My Book

_____

The Pen

One hen went fast.

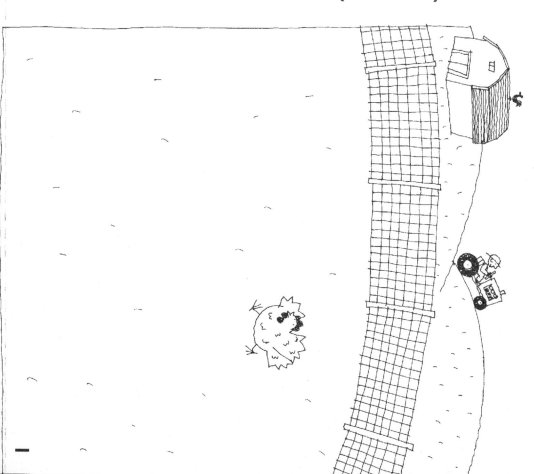

1

Three dogs went fast.

(Fold Line)

Two cats went fast.

Name

Make Them the Same

✂ Cut out the shapes at the bottom of the page.

Paste them on to make the pictures match.

Off We Go—See What We Know! 39

Name _____

That Tickles!

✏️ Trace the letters. Draw a line from each letter

to a picture whose name starts like  🐟 .

✏️   f   f   f   f   f

 Off We Go—See What We Know!   **41**

Name _____

Pass the Soap!

✏️ Trace the letters. Draw a line from each letter

to a picture whose name starts like 🦭 .

S   S   S   S   S

42   Off We Go—See What We Know!

Name _____

Feel the Sand

✏️ **Think of each beginning sound. Write f or s.**

✏️ **Draw a line from each letter you wrote to the correct umbrella.**

Off We Go—See What We Know!

43

Name

Tasty Treats

✏️▷ Circle the word that names each picture.

🖍️▷ Then draw something for the table that begins

like 🐟 or 🦭 .

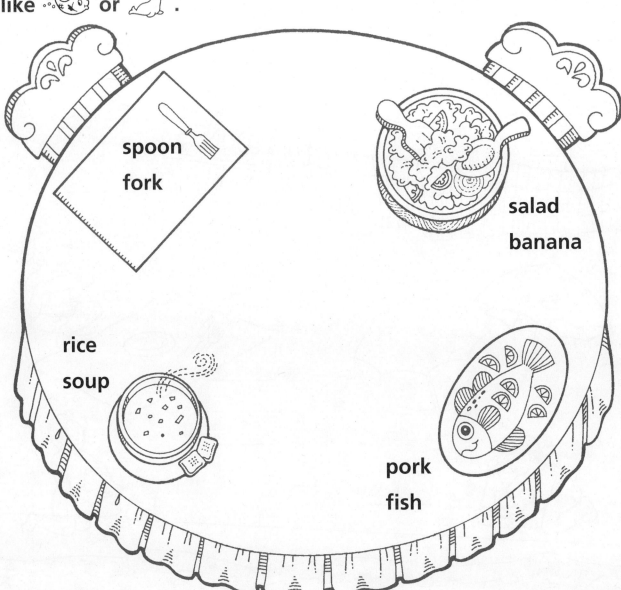

spoon

fork

salad

banana

rice

soup

pork

fish

✏️▷ Write a word that names your picture.

Name

Puzzle Pictures

h

Color in each space that has a picture whose name begins like .

What hidden picture did you find?

Colorful Q

Name

q

Color in each space that has a picture whose name begins like .

What hidden letter did you find?

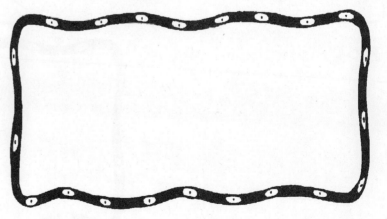

Name

What Do You See?

✎ **Think of each beginning sound. Write h or qu.**

🖍 **Color brown the pictures whose names begin like .**

Color yellow the pictures whose names begin like 👑 .

Name

Help the Queen!

Read the story.

The **queen has** a rip!

The **queen's heel** tips!

Help! Quick!

 Choose one of the pictures.

Draw how it can help the queen. Label your picture.

Name _____

Seaside Sights

✎ Think of each beginning sound. Circle the
word that names each picture.

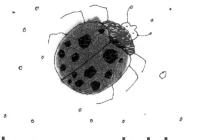

hug   ladybug

beef   leaf

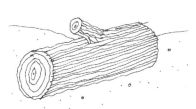

log   dog

leg   peg

lobster   robber

ramp   lamp

Name

Take a Look!

 W

 Think of each beginning sound. Circle the word that names each picture.

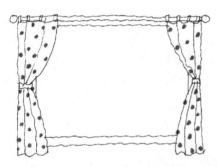

window   **yellow**

wagon   **dragon**

sandal   **windmill**

good   **wood**

last   **wasp**

water   **tunnel**

Use Your Senses

✐ Think of each beginning sound. Write **l** or **w**.

✐ Draw a line from each letter you wrote to the correct jar.

 Off We Go—See What We Know! **51**

Name

See Three Dogs

Read the story.

1. **Look!** Three dogs **wear** hats!

2. Three dogs **leap**!

3. Three dogs **wave**!

4. The dogs make me **laugh**!

 Write something the dogs could do that begins like 🦁 **or** 🐛 **.**

_____

- -

_____

4

Baby Hog, land!
Nice sand!

(Fold Line)

This Is My Book

Run Fast!

Baby Hog sees.

4

Baby Hog, see the sand.

(Fold Line)

Baby Hog, run fast!

Name _____

Do You See?

Read the story.

 **Draw what the baby will do next.**

We have a baby.

Our baby jogs with the dog.

Run fast!

See our baby pat the cat.

Pat my nose.

Write about your picture.

_____

- -

_____

- -

_____

Name

Body Language

 Draw eyes, a nose, and a mouth on the person. Then draw ears and hands.

eyes	nose
ears	hands
mouth	

 Write the name of each part.

Draw a line from each label to the picture.

Name _____

All About Me

Draw a picture of yourself.

Finish the sentences about you.

My name is _____.

I like to play _____.

I like to eat _____.

 Cut out the picture. Hang it where others can see it.

Off We Go—See What We Know! **55**

Name

Make a 1-2-3-4 Book

✂ Cut out these things and paste them in your Number Book.

| 1 | 🐷🐷🐷 | 4 |

| 🐱 | 2 | 3 | 🐕 |

☐ Did I put a number on each page of my book?

☐ Did I put an animal name on each page?

☐ Did I make the right number of animals?

5

Name _____

Spring, Summer, Fall

| l | r |

✏️ **Think of each ending sound. Write l or r.**

April	July
⬅ _____	_____
May	**August**
_____	_____
June	**September**
⬅ _____	_____

🖍 **Color blue the pictures whose names end like** ✳️ **.**

Color orange the pictures whose names end like 🫙 **.**

Then read the names of the months with your teacher.

Underline the months that end with the sound for l or r.

 Growing & Changing **67**

Name

Boxes to Fill

 Draw a line from the picture to the word
it goes with.

tool

 bear

wheel

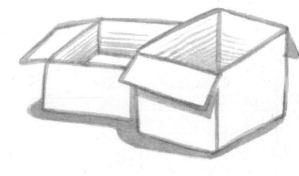

 Write a word that ends like ⊛ or 🫙 to finish
the last sentence.

I have one **car**.

_____

- -

You have one _____ .

 Draw a picture to go with your sentence.

4

We fit!
We fill it!

(Fold Line)

We will not all fit.

This Is My Book

_____

Will We Fit?

1

Sit, sit!
We will fit.

3

(Fold Line)

We will not all fit.

2

Name _____

One, Two, Three

✏️ **Choose a word from the box to finish each sentence. Draw and write an ending for the story.**

for	it
will	is

❶

It _____ not for the dog.

❷

Is _____ for the cat?

❸

It is _____ you.

But _____ three fit?

❹

_____
- - - - - - - - - - - - -
_____
- - - - - - - - - - - - -
_____
- - - - - - - - - - - - -
_____

Growing & Changing **69**

Name

Fun All Year

Can you name the months of the year?

January	February	March	April
May	June	July	August
September	October	November	December

 Write an ending to each sentence. The pictures will give you ideas. Draw a picture for each answer.

In April and May, I smell a

_____

_____ .

In July and August, I play with a

_____

_____ .

In October and November, I grow a

_____

_____ .

Name

My Special Things

✏️ Write a list of things you like to save and keep.

① _____

② _____

③ _____

④ _____

🖍️ In the boxes, draw pictures of your things.

✂️ Cut them out and paste them to the shelf.

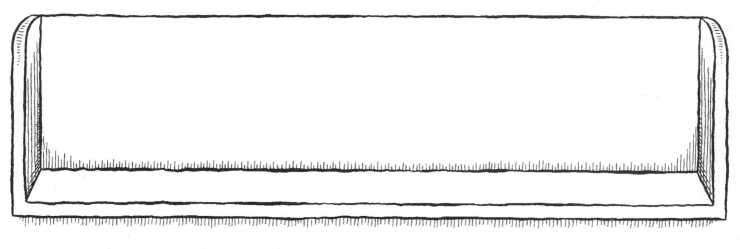

Name

What Would They Say?

✏️ Write **Me too!** or **Not me!** in the speech balloons to show what the animals and children would say.

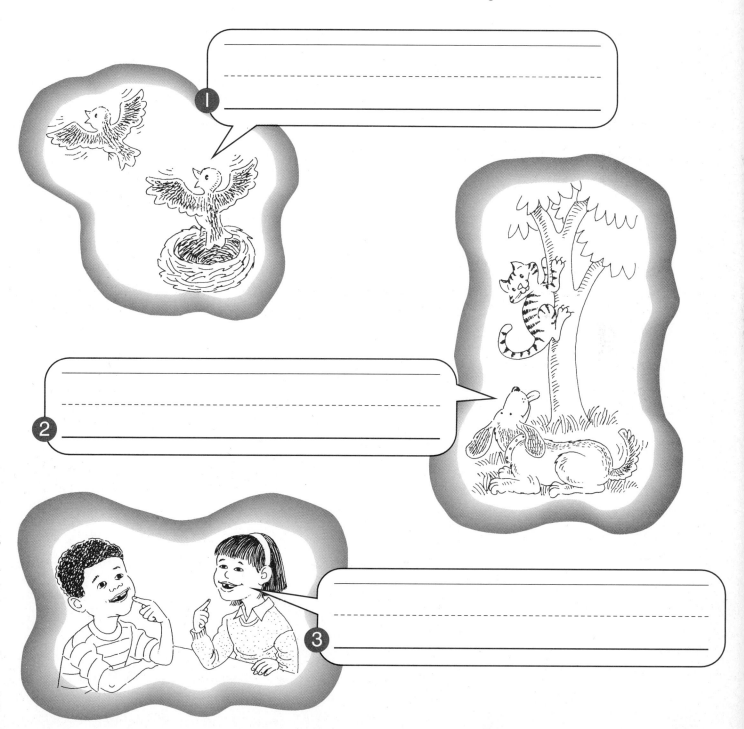

Name

Chick Takes a Look

✏️ Draw lines from the big chick to things whose names end with the same sound as 🐥.

Look!

Name

Duckling's Worm

✏️ Draw lines from the big worm to things whose names end with the same sound as .

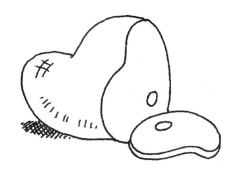

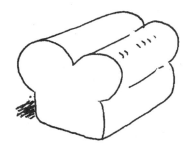

worm

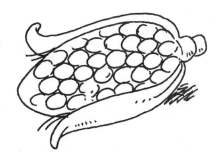

Name _____

Busy Birds

| k | m |

✏️ **See what the birds have. Think of each**

ending sound. Write k or m.

✏️ **Circle the things that end like** 🍴 .

Mark an X on the things that end like .

Name _____

Go, Duck!

✏️ Draw a line to connect each sentence to the picture it goes with.

1 I **walk**.   **2** I **look**.   **3** I **swim**.   **4** I **dream**.

✏️ Write a word that ends like or to finish the sentence.

_____

- -

I will _____ with the .

🖍️ Draw a picture to go with your sentence.

Name

For a Growing Baby

b

 Think of each ending sound.

Circle the word that names the picture.

tub

tug

bib

big

cry

crib

wet

web

Name

A Guest for Chick

✏️ **Think of each ending sound.**

Circle the word that names the picture.

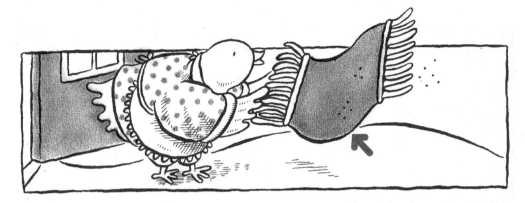

rug
run

low
log

pig
pit

hug
hum

The Chick and the Duckling
PHONICS AND SPELLING
Final Consonants: *b, g*

Name _____

Help the Duckling

b   g

✏️ **Think of each ending sound. Write b or g.**

✏️ **Help the Duckling find his way to the stream.**

Follow the path with pictures whose names end like **.**

The Chick and the Duckling
PHONICS AND SPELLING
Final Consonants: *b, g*

Name

Dig This!

✂ **Read and cut out the speech balloons.**

Paste them beside the pictures to show what the

chicks would say.

I **sob**.   We **jog**.   I **dig**.

✏️ **Write a word that ends like** 🛏 **or** 🐕 **to finish the sentence.**

_____

Will you _____ with me, 🐤 ?

🖍 **Draw a picture to go with your sentence.**

"But I am big!" said
Sam Ham.

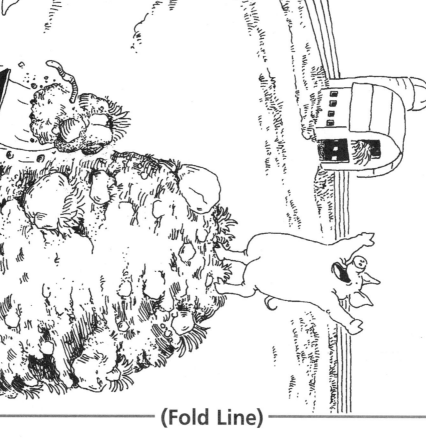

(Fold Line)

This Is My Book

Me Too!

"I am big," said Big Pig.
"I will run."
"I will run too," said Sam Ham.

"I am big," said Big Pig.
"I will dig."

"I will not dig," said
Sam Ham.

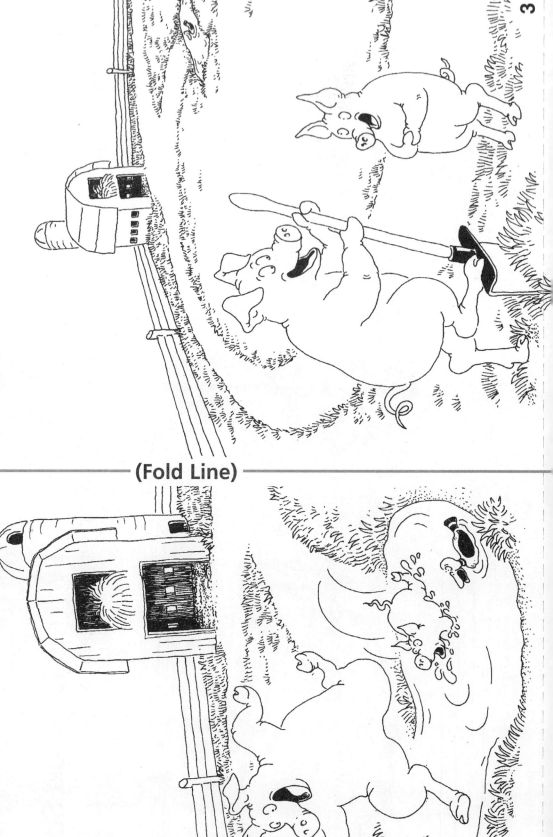

(Fold Line)

"I am big," said Big Pig.
"I will jump."

"I will jump too," said
Sam Ham.

Name _____

Not Me!

✂ **Read the story. Cut out and paste each picture in the box where it belongs.**

① ▭	② ▭
Duck came to see Dog. "I am Duck," he said. Dog said, "I am Dog."	Cat came to see Duck and Dog. "I am Cat," he said.
③ ▭	④ ▭
"I will jump," said Duck. "Me too," said Dog.	"Not me," said Cat. "I will not jump!"

✏️ **What do you think Cat will do now? Write about Cat.**

_____

- -

_____

_____

- -

_____

_____

- -

_____

_____

- -

_____

Name

Who Are You?

| I am = I'm | I will = I'll |

 Write the sentences again, using I'm and I'll.

Then color the pictures.

I am a dog. I will run.

_____

- -

_____

I am a cat. I will jump.

_____

- -

_____

I am a chick. I will run and jump, too!

_____

- -

_____

_____

- -

_____

Name

Lost!

Help the baby animals find their mothers. Draw a line from each animal to its mother. Then write the animal names next to their pictures.

piglet

calf

duck

duckling

pig

cow

Name

What's Baking?

✏️ The words name the pictures. Write a
letter to finish each word.

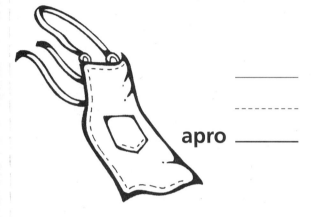

apro _____

pa _____

spoo _____

ma _____

🖍️ It's time for pumpkin pie! Draw a plate.

Use a color whose name ends with **n**.

The plate is

_____

_____.

Name

In the Garden

| d | n |

 Think of each ending sound. Write d or n.

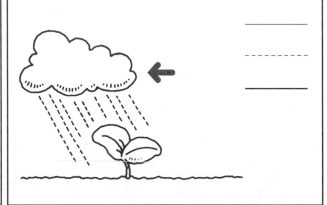

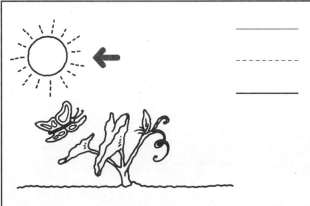

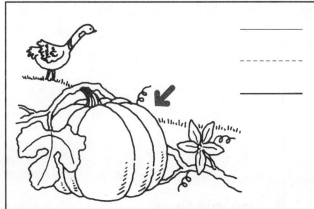

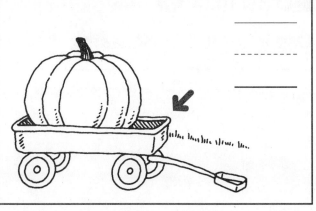

 Color green the pictures that end like 🛏 **.**

Color brown the pictures that end like 🧰 **.**

Name _____

What's Outside?

| d | n |

✏️ **Write each word next to the picture it goes with.**

| moon | garden | wood | road |

🖍 **Draw a picture of something you might see outside.**

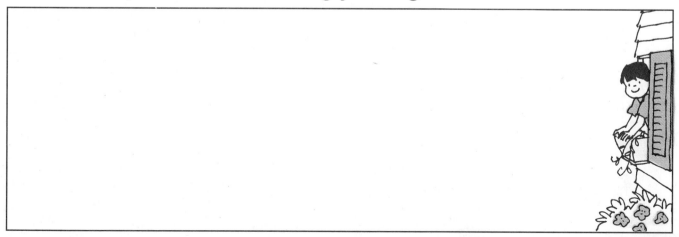

Growing and Changing **91**

Name

Skip to the Jeep

p

✏ Write a letter to finish each word.

🖍 Help the girl go to the jeep. Connect the
things whose names end like .

soa _____

shee _____

do _____

bir _____

cu _____

be _____

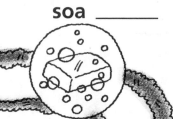

ma _____

10

te _____

lam _____

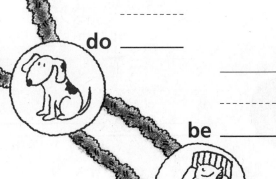

jeep

Name

Max's Birthday

✂ Read the story. Cut out and paste each
picture in the box where it belongs.

①

A box!

②

A fox!

③

An ox!

④

Max is six!

Name _____

In the Yard

✏️ **Think of each ending sound. Write p or x.**

✏️ **Circle each picture that ends like .**

Mark an X on each picture that ends like 6.

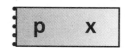

Name

Pumpkin Time

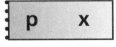

| p | x |

🖎 **Draw a line to connect each picture to the sentence it goes with.**

The **pup** jumps up.   The **box** is for you.   It is time to **scoop**.

🖎 **Write two words that end like 🖼 or 6️⃣ to finish the sentence.**

_____

- -

I have a _____ for the dog and a

_____

- -

_____ for the pup.

🖍 **Draw a picture to go with your sentence.**

And then, up came my plant!

(Fold Line)

This Is My Book

A Plant for Me!

I will put six seeds in a tin.

One weed, two weeds, three weeds!

(Fold Line)

Then I will feed my seeds.

Out, Dog!

Use the words to write a sentence about each picture. Then color the pictures.

six	We	in	plants.	put

_____

_____

_____

came	dog	in.	a	Then

_____

_____

_____

went	The	out	fast.	dog

_____

_____

_____

Name

One, Two, Three, Jump!

✐ **Read the story and circle the word endings. Then draw a line from each sentence to the picture it matches.**

1 I am planting.

2 The cat is jumping.

3 The baby jumps too.

4 I planted all my plants.

5 Then I jumped too!

Name

Garden Work

 Color the picture.

✏️ Finish the sentences. Use the words from the box.

❶ The man _____ a hole.

picks
digs
plants

❷ The girl _____ the seed.

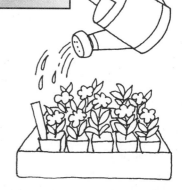

❸ The boy _____ an apple.

Name

Making Little-Big Cards

 Plan what you will draw on your cards.

Little	Big

Did you?

☐ Did you draw two animals or plants in each set?

☐ Did you make one little and one big?

Name of Book

_____

- -

_____

Name of Book

_____

- -

_____

Name of Book

_____

- -

_____

Name of Book

_____

- -

_____

Name of Book

_____

- -

_____

Name of Book

_____

- -

_____

Name of Book

_____

- -

_____

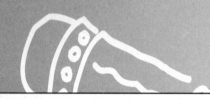

MY FAVORITE STORIES

Name of Book

_____

- -

_____

Name of Book

_____

- -

_____

Name of Book

_____

- -

_____

Name of Book

_____

- -

_____

Name of Book

_____

- -

_____

Name of Book

_____

- -

_____

Name of Book

_____

- -

_____

Name of Book

_____

- - - - - - - - - - - - - - - - - - - -

_____

Name of Book

_____

- - - - - - - - - - - - - - - - - - - -

_____

Name of Book

_____

- - - - - - - - - - - - - - - - - - - -

_____

Name of Book

_____

- - - - - - - - - - - - - - - - - - - -

_____

Name of Book

_____

- - - - - - - - - - - - - - - - - - - -

_____

Name of Book

_____

- - - - - - - - - - - - - - - - - - - -

_____

Name of Book

_____

- - - - - - - - - - - - - - - - - - - -

_____

MY FAVORITE STORIES

Name of Book

_____

Name of Book

_____

_____

Name of Book

_____

_____

Name of Book

_____

_____

Name of Book

_____

_____

Name of Book

_____

_____

Name of Book

_____

_____

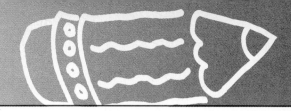

Trace and write the letters.

Aa Aa

Bb Bb

Cc Cc

Dd Dd

Ee Ee

Ff Ff

Gg Gg

McDougal, Littell 1993 Handwriting (continuous stroke)

✏ **Trace and write the letters.**

Hh Hh

Ii Ii

Jj Jj

Kk Kk

Ll Ll

Mm Mm

McDougal, Littell 1993 Handwriting (continuous stroke)

✐ **Trace and write the letters.**

Nn Nn

Oo Oo

Pp Pp

Qq Qq

Rr Rr

Ss Ss

Tt Tt

✏️ **Trace and write the letters.**

Uu Uu

Vv Vv

Ww Ww

Xx Xx

Yy Yy

Zz Zz

McDougal, Littell 1993 Handwriting (continuous stroke)

 **Trace and write the letters.**

Aa Aa

Bb Bb

Cc Cc

Dd Dd

Ee Ee

Ff Ff

Gg Gg

McDougal, Littell 1993 Handwriting (ball and stick)

✏️ **Trace and write the letters.**

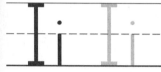

Hh Hh

Ii Ii

Jj Jj

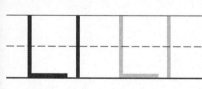

Kk Kk

Ll Ll

Mm Mm

McDougal, Littell 1993 Handwriting (ball and stick)

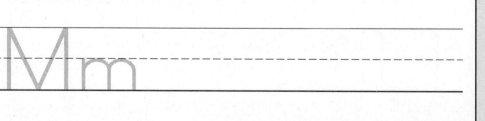

✏️ **Trace and write the letters.**

Nn Nn

Oo Oo

Pp Pp

Qq Qq

Rr Rr

Ss Ss

Tt Tt

✏️ **Trace and write the letters.**

U u U u

V v V v

W w W w

X x X x

Y y Y y

Z z Z z

McDougal, Littell 1993 Handwriting (ball and stick)

A A A B B C C D D

E E E F F G G H H

I I J J K K L L M

M N N O O P P Q Q

R R S S T T U U V

V W W X X Y Y Z Z

fold

fold

d	d	c	c	b	b	a	a	a
h	h	g	g	f	f	e	e	e
m	l	l	k	k	j	j	i	i
q	q	p	p	o	o	n	n	m
v	u	u	t	t	s	s	r	r
z	z	y	y	x	x	w	w	v

WHEN THIS BOX IS FULL	MY FIVE SENSES	ONE RED ROOSTER	ANNIE, BEA, AND CHI CHI DOLORES
High-Frequency Words	High-Frequency Words	High-Frequency Words	High-Frequency Words
but	a	and	all
?	?	?	?
for	baby	cat	I
?	?	?	?
is	have	dog	jump
?	?	?	?
it	my	fast	run
?	?	?	?
not	our	one	the
?	?	?	?
will	see	three	time
?	?	?	?
you	we	two	up
?	?	?	?
	with	went	
?	?	?	?
?	?	?	?
?	?	?	?

ANNIE, BEA, AND CHI CHI DOLORES	ONE RED ROOSTER	MY FIVE SENSES	WHEN THIS BOX IS FULL
?	?	?	?
?	?	?	?
?	?	?	?
?	?	?	?
?	?	?	?
?	?	?	?
?	?	?	?
?	?	?	?
?	?	?	?
?	?	?	?

NUMBER WORDS	COLOR WORDS	PUMPKIN PUMPKIN High-Frequency Words	THE CHICK AND THE DUCKLING High-Frequency Words
one	red	in	am
?	?	?	?
two	yellow	out	came
?	?	?	?
three	blue	plant	he
?	?	?	?
four	green	put	me
?	?	?	?
five	pink	six	said
?	?	?	?
six	purple	then	too
?	?	?	?
seven	white		
?	?	?	?
eight	brown		
?	?	?	?
nine	black		
?	?	?	?
ten	orange		
?	?	?	?

THE CHICK AND THE DUCKLING	PUMPKIN PUMPKIN	COLOR WORDS	NUMBER WORDS
?	?	?	?
?	?	?	?
?	?	?	?
?	?	?	?
?	?	?	?
?	?	?	?
?	?	?	?
?	?	?	?
?	?	?	?
?	?	?	?

with	one	all
but	three	I
for	two	jump
is	went	run
it	a	the
not	baby	time
will	have	up
you	my	and
am	our	cat
came	see	dog
he	we	fast

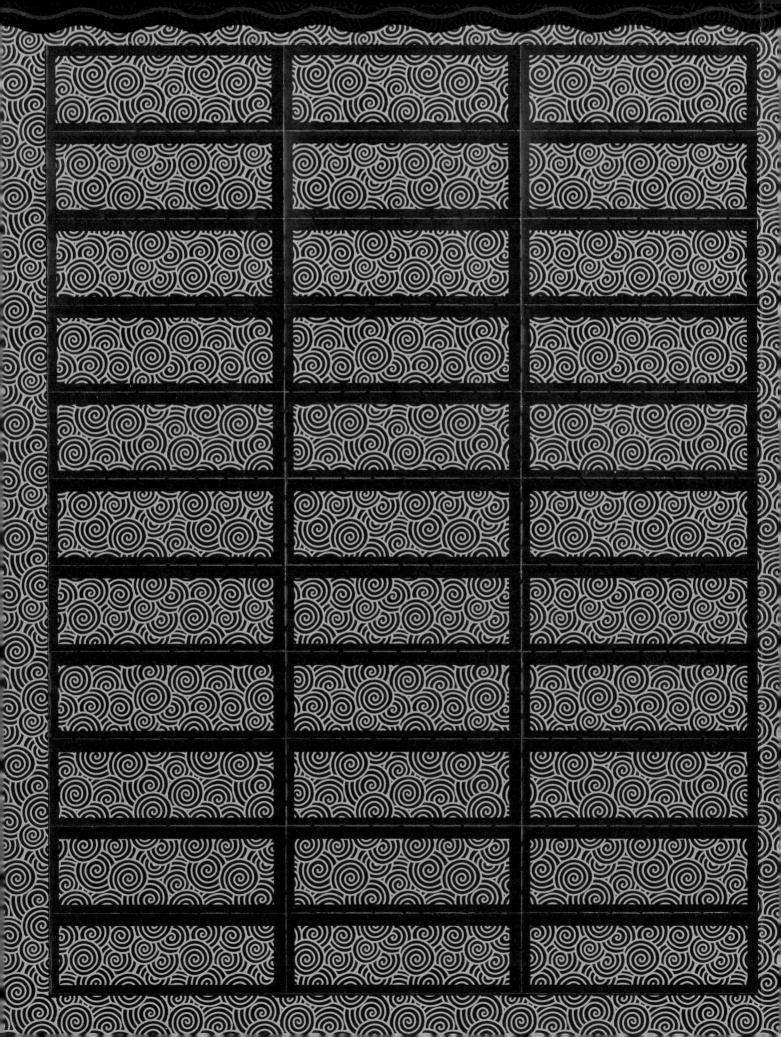

put	in	me
six	out	said
then	plant	too

red	yellow	blue
green		brown
orange	Color the back of each card to match the color word.	black
pink	purple	white

1	2	3	4	5
one	two	three	four	five
6	7	8	9	10
six	seven	eight	nine	ten

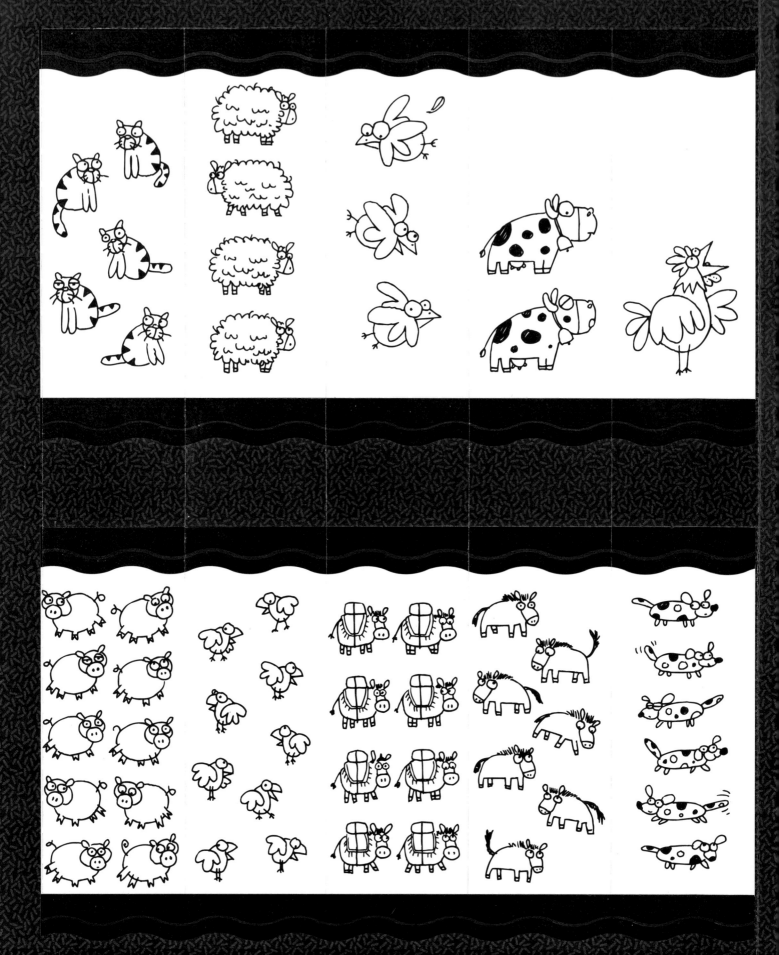